Contents

Discovering caves

Do you like climbing, swimming, and exploring? You could think about becoming a **spelunker**! A spelunker is someone who explores caves.

LANDFOR

Pam Rosenberg

www.raintreepublishers.co.uk
Visit our website to find out more information about Raintree books.

To order:
Phone 0845 6044371
Fax +44 (0) 1865 312263
Email myorders@raintreepublishers.co.uk

Customers from outside the UK please telephone +44 1865 312262

Raintree is an imprint of Capstone Global Library Limited, a company incorporated in England and Wales having its registered office at 7 Pilgrim Street, London, EC4V 6LB – Registered company number: 6695582

First published in hardback in 2012
Paperback edition first published in 2013

Edited by Rebecca Rissman, Dan Nunn, and Sian Smith
Designed by Joanna Hinton Malivoire
Picture research by Elizabeth Alexander
Production by Victoria Fitzgerald
Originated by Capstone Global Library
Printed and bound in China by CTPS

ISBN 978 1 406 22566 2 (hardback)
15 14 13 12 11
10 9 8 7 6 5 4 3 2 1

ISBN 978 1 406 22573 0 (paperback)
16 15 14 13 12
10 9 8 7 6 5 4 3 2 1

British Library Cataloguing in Publication Data
Rosenberg, Pam.
Cave crawlers. -- (Landform adventurers)
1. Caves--Juvenile literature. 2. Spelunkers--Juvenile literature.
I. Title II. Series
551.4'47-dc22

Acknowledgements
We would like to thank the following for permission to reproduce photographs: Alamy pp. 10 (© Bert de Ruiter), 12 (© Robbie Shone), 15 (© Gavin Newman), 19 (© Ladi Kirn) 24 (© Robbie Shone); Corbis pp. 6 (© David Sutherland), 8 (© Ashley Cooper), 18 (© Sasson Tiram/ Reuters); Getty Images pp. 7 (Todd Gipstein/National Geographic), 14 (Stephen Alvarez/National Geographic), 25 (Danita Delimont/Gallo Images), 26 (Stephen Alvarez/ National Geographic); iStockphoto p. 11 top (© Günay Mutlu); Photolibrary pp. 4 (Boomer Jerritt), 5 (Philippe Crochet), 17 (John Cancalosi), 20 (Juan Carlos Munoz), 28 (A Demotes/Photononstop); Science Photo Library pp. 21 (Pascal Goetgheluck), 29 (Martin Bond); Shutterstock pp. 9 (© Stephanie Coffman), 11 bottom (© Christophe Testi), 13, 16 (© Grigory Kubatyan), 22 (© Sági Elemér), 27 (© Songquan Deng). Cover photograph of a caver in Ogof Ffynnon Ddu, South Wales reproduced with permission of Alamy (© Anthony Baker).

Every effort has been made to contact copyright holders of material reproduced in this book. Any omissions will be rectified in subsequent printings if notice is given to the publisher.

Some words are shown in bold, **like this**. You can find out what they mean by looking in the glossary.

Caves are like pockets in the Earth. Some caves are just big enough for a person to fit inside. Others stretch underground for many kilometres.

Caves form in different ways. Most caves are formed when rock is worn away by water.

Some caves are formed when **lava** flows from a **volcano**. The top layer hardens, while lava flows underneath. When the lava stops flowing, a cave is left under the top, hard layer.

This cave in Hawaii was formed by lava.

Cave explorers

You have to be strong to be a **spelunker**. You must be ready to crawl through small openings, or swim through ice-cold water. You might need to use ropes to climb steep rock walls. Are you ready for the challenge?

DANGER AHEAD!

Caves can be dangerous places. Never go **caving** alone. Make sure you have at least one adult with you when you go exploring.

Some people like **spelunking** so much that they make it their job. They combine science and **caving**. These people are called **speleologists**.

What do speleologists need?

Helmets

Lights

Warm clothing

Sturdy boots

Speleologists need to use proper safety equipment.

Rocks and water

Some **speleologists** explore caves to study rocks. If they're lucky, they might see **stalagmites** or **stalactites**! Speleologists use rock hammers and other tools to learn more about how caves formed.

Stalactite is spelt with a "c". Stalactites hang from the ceiling.

Stalagmite is spelt with a "g". Stalagmites form on the ground.

Some caves are filled with water. These caves are dangerous! People need special training to explore them. They also need special tools such as air tanks and **fins**.

Some caves even have waterfalls.

Powerful lights are needed to explore underwater caves.

Who lives in caves?

Speleologists don't just study rocks. They study living things, too. During the day bats hang from cave ceilings. They fly out when it gets dark. Night-time is when they find insects to eat.

Carlsbad Caverns, New Mexico, USA

CAVE FACT

Make sure you wear boots when you explore bat caves. The cave floor will be covered in **guano**, or bat poo! Guano is good for helping plants grow.

There are some animals that spend their whole lives in caves. They are blind. Can you guess why?

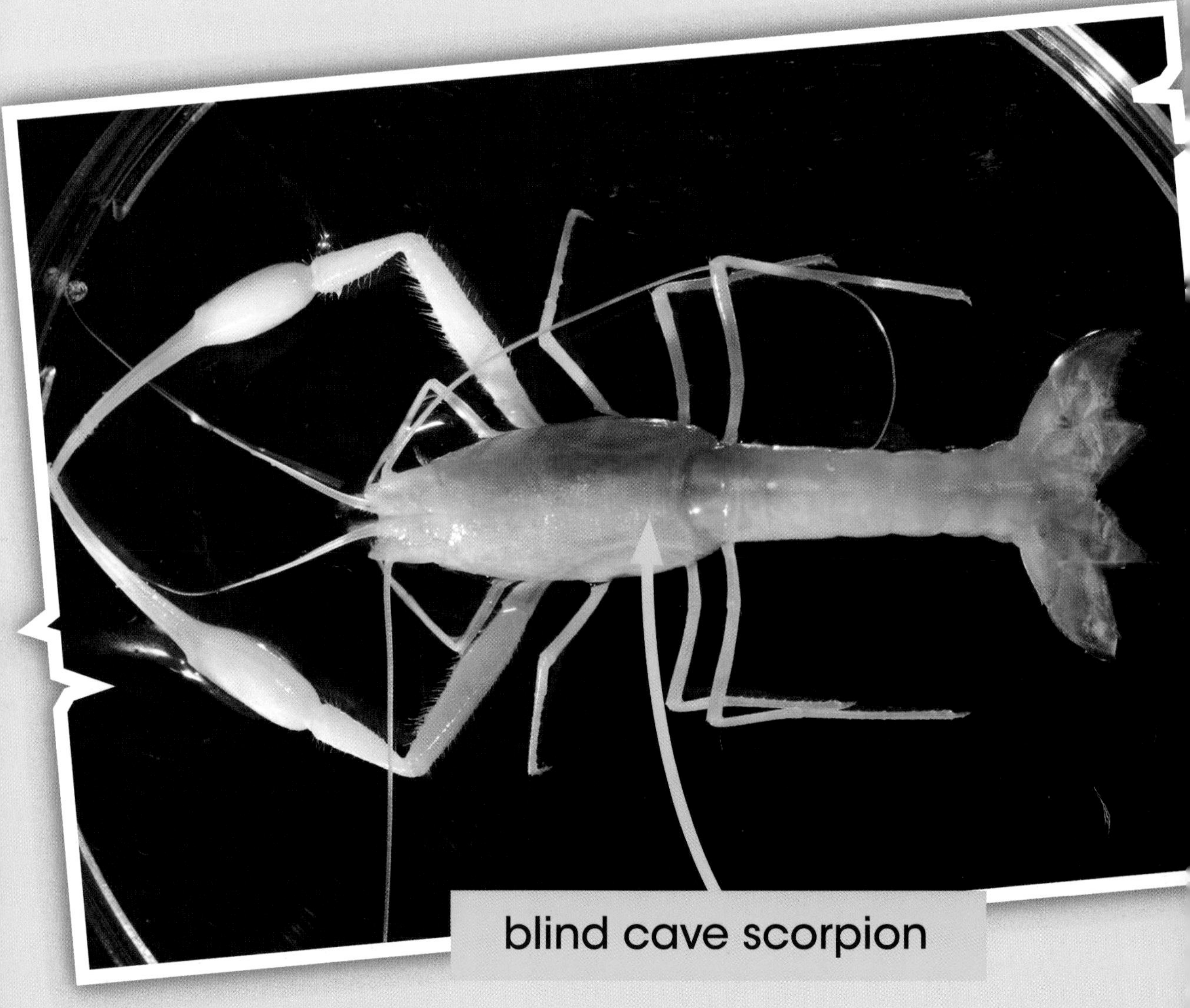

blind cave scorpion

The answer is – they don't need to see because it is too dark in caves! They use their other senses to get around.

Many people lived in caves thousands of years ago. How do we know this? **Speleologists** have found drawings and human **artefacts** in caves. Cameras are important tools for these cave explorers. They take pictures of the artefacts to study later.

CAVE FACT

Piles of **ancient** human poo can tell speleologists a lot about people who lived in caves many years ago. The poo can tell us what ancient people ate.

Amazing caves

Caves can be found all over the world. Some are known for their size. Others have underground waterfalls or lakes. Some caves really *are* cool to explore – they are formed in ice!

Ice cave in Dobsina, Slovakia

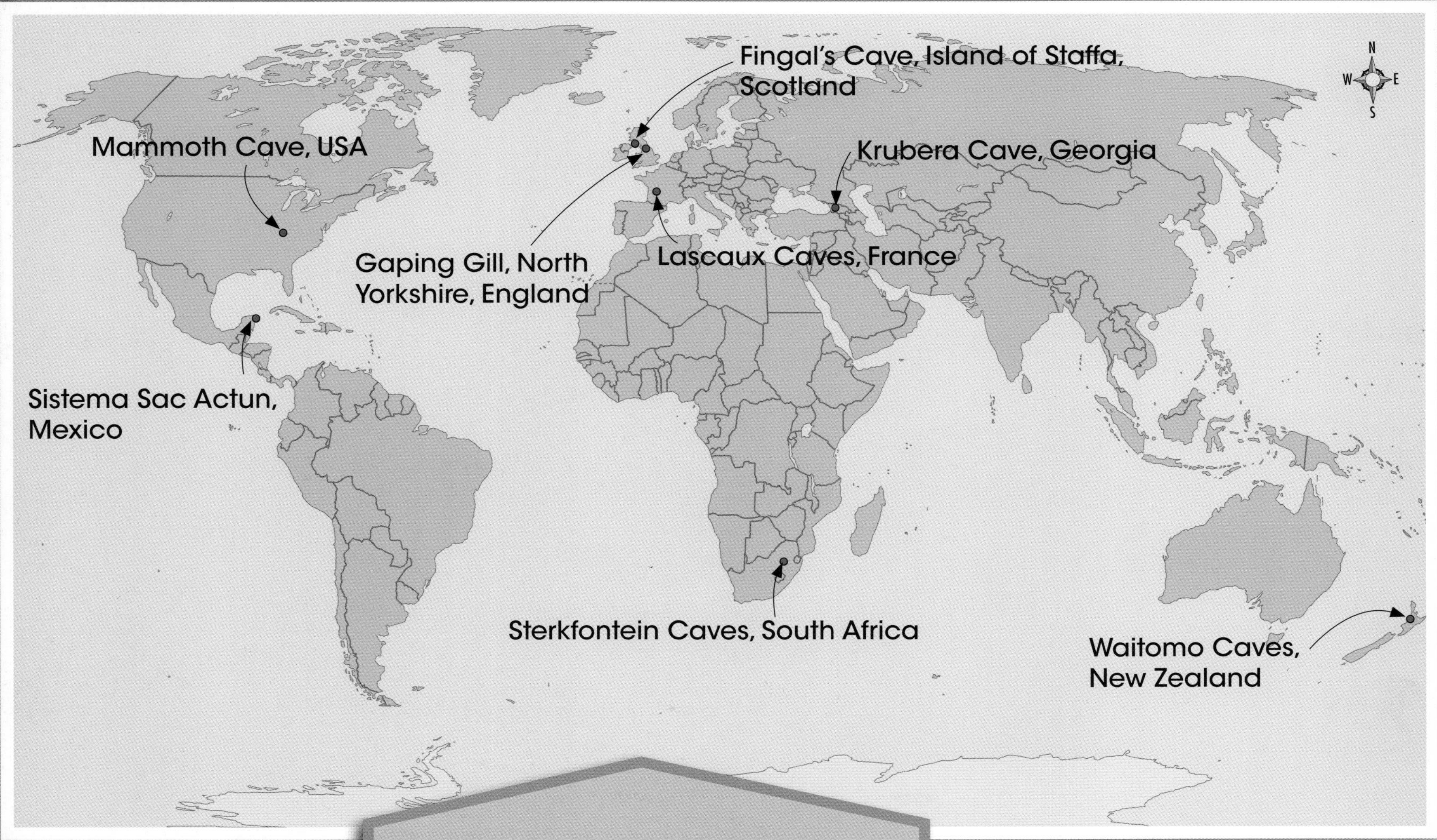

Some of the greatest caves in the world are shown on this map.

Now that's long!

Mammoth Cave in Kentucky, in the United States, is the world's longest known cave. More than 591 kilometres of passages have been explored. That's more than half the length of Britain!

People visit Mammoth Cave to see the amazing **stalactites** and **stalagmites**.

Deep underground

Krubera Cave is the world's deepest cave. It is found in the country of Georgia. The cave is 2,191 metres deep. You could fit four Empire State Buildings in a hole that deep and still have room left over!

This climber is going down into Krubera Cave on a rope.

New York City, USA
Empire State Building

Are you ready to explore?

Does being a cave crawler sound like fun to you? Then learn as much as you can about caves. Stay active so your body gets strong. Go swimming, hiking, and join a climbing club.

Ask your parents to help you find a group that explores caves in your area. Start exploring and you may be a **speleologist** one day!

Glossary

ancient hundreds or thousands of years old

artefact object made or changed by humans

caving the sport of exploring caves

fins long, flat rubber shoes that help divers to swim. Fins are also called "flippers".

guano bat or seabird poo

lava hot, liquid rock that comes out of a volcano when it erupts

speleologist scientist who studies and explores caves

spelunker person who explores caves as a hobby

spelunking sport of exploring caves

stalactite piece of rock shaped like an icicle that hangs from the ceiling of a cave

stalagmite piece of rock shaped like an icicle that sticks up from the floor of a cave

volcano vent in the Earth's crust, or outer layer, through which lava, ash, and gas erupt

Find out more

Find out

Where can you find the Ceiling of the Red Cows?

Books

Caves, Kimberly M Hutmacher (Capstone, 2011)

Caves and Crevices, Sharon Katz Cooper (Raintree, 2010)

I Wonder Why Stalactites Hang Down?, Jackie Gaff (Kingfisher, 2004)

Websites

library.thinkquest.org/J0112123/
Find out about caves and some of the animals that might live there.

www.canyonsworldwide.com/crystals/index.html
Look inside a crystal cave using this website.

www.cave-exploring.com/Cave%20Types.htm
This website helps you learn about different kinds of cave and the basic rules of caving.

www.lascaux.culture.fr/#/en/00.xml
Discover pictures of the cave art found at Lascaux in France.

Index